KIM KARDASHIAN WEST

JESSICA RUSICK

Checkerboard
Library

An Imprint of Abdo Publishing
abdobooks.com

ABDOBOOKS.COM

Published by Abdo Publishing, a division of ABDO, PO Box 398166, Minneapolis, Minnesota 55439.
Copyright © 2020 by Abdo Consulting Group, Inc. International copyrights reserved in all countries.
No part of this book may be reproduced in any form without written permission from the publisher.
Checkerboard Library™ is a trademark and logo of Abdo Publishing.

Printed in the United States of America, North Mankato, Minnesota
052019
092019

THIS BOOK CONTAINS
RECYCLED MATERIALS

Design and Production: Mighty Media, Inc.
Editor: Megan Borgert-Spaniol
Cover Photograph: Shutterstock Images
Interior Photographs: Alamy, pp. 27, 29 (top); AP Images, pp. 5, 9, 17, 19, 21, 23, 29 (bottom left); Seth
Poppel/Yearbook Library, p. 7; Shutterstock Images, pp. 11, 13, 15, 25, 28 (top, bottom left, bottom right),
29 (bottom right)

Library of Congress Control Number: 2018966246

Publisher's Cataloging-in-Publication Data
Names: Rusick, Jessica, author.
Title: Kim Kardashian West / by Jessica Rusick
Description: Minneapolis, Minnesota : Abdo Publishing, 2020 | Series: Checkerboard biographies |
    Includes online resources and index.
Identifiers: ISBN 9781532119415 (lib. bdg.) | ISBN 9781532173875 (ebook)
Subjects: LCSH: West, Kim Kardashian, 1980- --Juvenile literature. | Television personalities--Biography--
    Juvenile literature. | Women entrepreneurs--Biography--Juvenile literature. | Socialites--Biography--
    Juvenile literature.
Classification: DDC 791.45028902 [B]--dc23

CONTENTS

CHAPTER 1

SOCIAL SENSATION

Kim Kardashian West first became famous for her role on the popular reality TV show *Keeping Up with the Kardashians*. Since then, her career has expanded far beyond a single TV show. Kardashian West is an internationally recognized celebrity, **entrepreneur**, and social media star. Her beauty company, KKW Beauty, makes millions of dollars a year. Her **selfies** regularly get millions of likes. Kardashian West's fans see her as a lifestyle icon.

Kardashian West built her success on sharing her life with fans. From TV to social media, Kardashian West prided herself on being open and honest. At times, this was challenging. People did not always approve of her choices. But Kardashian West was able to ignore her critics and stay true to herself.

From a young age, Kardashian West was taught to value hard work. This early lesson would help her throughout her career. Sharing her life has not always been easy on Kardashian West. But it has made her the successful woman she is today.

Keeping Up with the Kardashians won best reality series at the MTV Movie & TV Awards in June 2018. Kardashian West and her mom, Kris Jenner, accepted the award.

CHAPTER 2

WILLING TO WORK

Kimberly Noel Kardashian was born on October 21, 1980 in Beverly Hills, California. Her mother, Kris, was a **socialite** and store owner. Her father, Robert, was a lawyer. Kim had two sisters and a brother.

In 1989, Kim's parents divorced. In 1991, her mother married Olympic athlete Caitlyn Jenner. Jenner was known as Bruce before coming out as **transgender** in 2015. Kim gained four step-siblings from Jenner's previous marriage. She would later welcome two half-sisters. Kim lived with her mom, Jenner, and their family in Calabasas, California.

In 1994, Kim began attending the all-girls Catholic high school Marymount in Los Angeles, California. She said this strict school helped give her a strong work **ethic**. In high school, she held jobs at a clothing store and her father Robert's business.

While working, Kim also pursued her interests in fashion and beauty. She loved to sell clothes and shoes on the website eBay. She also loved makeup. Kim didn't know it then, but these interests would guide her later in life.

As a teenager, Kim had a strong sense of style. The clothes and shoes she sold online often came from her own closet!

CHAPTER 3

STYLIST TO STARS

In 1998, Kardashian graduated high school and attended Pierce College in Los Angeles. There, she studied communication. In 2000, she married music producer Damon Thomas. Kardashian remained in college for two more years, but she did not graduate.

In 2003, Kardashian faced a personal tragedy. Her father Robert died eight weeks after learning he had **cancer**. Kardashian would soon face another major life change. The following year, she and Thomas divorced.

Kardashian worked hard through these tough times. In 2004, she followed her interest in fashion by finding work as a personal stylist. The Kardashian family knew many celebrities. These celebrities became Kardashian's **clients**!

Kardashian's first client was the singer Brandy. Kardashian shopped and chose outfits for her. Soon, Kardashian gained more clients. She helped stars like Paris Hilton and Lindsay Lohan stay stylish.

AIRPORT CALL-OUT

Kardashian first realized she was famous while at an airport. She heard people calling her name and thought she knew them. But they were fans!

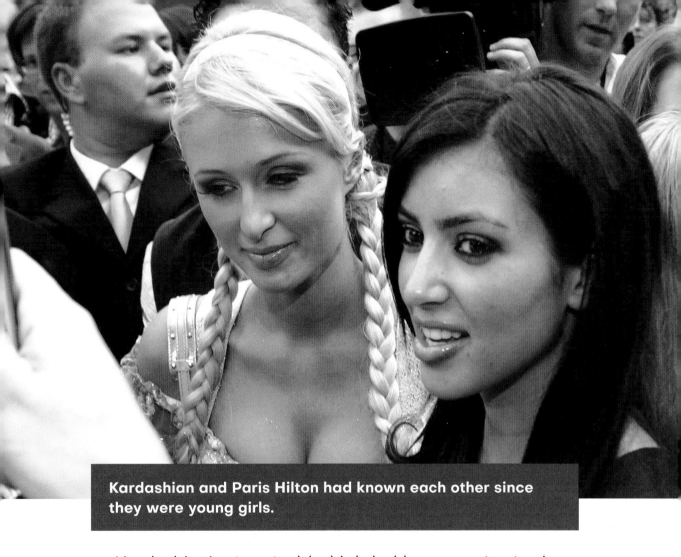

Kardashian and Paris Hilton had known each other since they were young girls.

Kardashian's star-studded job led her own star to rise. She was often photographed with her famous **clients**. She even appeared on TV. In 2006, Kardashian appeared on Hilton's reality show *The Simple Life*. Kardashian's growing fame helped reality TV producers see her **potential**.

CHAPTER 4

A NEW SHOW

Reality TV producers soon began talking to Kardashian about starring in a reality show. During these talks, Kardashian realized something. Any show of hers must also include her large, lively family! Kardashian felt she was far more interesting when surrounded by her mother, stepfather, and many siblings.

Producers worried that such a show would have too many characters. But soon they saw Kardashian was right. After filming test **footage** one night at a Kardashian family dinner, producers were hooked by the family's energy. They were ready to film a show.

In 2007, *Keeping Up with the Kardashians* **premiered** on the E! network. For the show, Kardashian agreed to share her life openly and honestly. This meant recording the good times and the bad. At first, Kardashian wasn't sure if *Keeping Up with the Kardashians* would last. But fans appreciated the show's drama. Many felt they could relate to the Kardashian family.

Over the following years, the show made Kardashian more popular than ever before. She starred on other

In 2006, Kardashian and her sisters Kourtney and Khloé opened a clothing store called DASH.

reality shows, such as *Dancing with the Stars*. She also lent her name to a number of products, including nail polish and jewelry. This means she was paid to **endorse** the products and pose in advertisements for them.

Kardashian's social media presence also brought her fame. In the first years of her show, she had a Twitter account and personal blog. Kardashian's real-time updates helped fans feel close to her.

However, not everyone was a fan of Kardashian. Her critics did not think she had a talent to justify her fame. Kardashian pushed back against this. She said it was a challenge to get people to care about her personal life. Indeed, some fans saw this as Kardashian's talent. She was an **entrepreneur**, able to turn her personal life into a brand.

The criticism did not hurt Kardashian's popularity. In 2011, *Keeping Up with the Kardashians* was E! network's most popular show. It regularly brought in millions of viewers a night.

That same year, Kardashian became engaged to basketball player Kris Humphries. The couple had been dating since December 2010.

> **My career came about at a time when social media was just starting, and I took advantage of it.**

The Kardashian sisters shared more than a TV show. In 2011, they launched the Kardashian Kollection, a fashion brand for Sears department stores.

E! announced plans to turn their wedding into a TV special. Fans everywhere were excited. But Kardashian would soon learn the challenges of publicizing her personal life.

CHAPTER 5

WEDDING & WOES

In 2011, **Kardashian and Humphries were set to be married.** Right before the wedding, Kardashian realized she was unhappy. But she did not want to disappoint her fans. So in August 2011, she married Humphries.

The marriage didn't last. Kardashian filed for divorce less than three months after the wedding. She told her fans she had gotten swept up in the TV show.

Critics accused Kardashian of planning the wedding and divorce to create drama and boost her show's **ratings**. After the divorce, an online **petition** called for an end to Kardashian's TV show. Those who signed it said Kardashian promoted a fake lifestyle.

These were all real moments. That's what makes us who we are. We share, we give, we love, and we are open!

In response, Kardashian said she had always been real. But sometimes she made mistakes. In the future, Kardashian would face more criticism. But she would also find more success and happiness than ever before.

Kardashian and Humphries' two-part, four-hour wedding special gave E! its highest ratings to date.

CHAPTER 6

FAMILY & FAME

In 2012, **Kardashian began dating rapper Kanye West.** The two had been friends since 2003. In 2013, Kanye revealed that he had been in love with Kardashian ever since they met! In June 2013, the couple had a daughter, North.

Kardashian and Kanye married in 2014. Kardashian changed her last name to West and made Kardashian her middle name. In 2015, the couple prepared for the birth of their second child, Saint.

As Kardashian West's family grew, her social media presence grew as well. In 2015, she had the second-most followed Instagram account, with 48.1 million followers. She was known for posting **selfies**. Some called her a selfie expert!

In May 2015, Kardashian West published many of her selfies in a book called *Selfish*. Her photos challenged widely held ideas about

> **I've always loved to interact with my fans online. Social media has allowed me to have relationships with people from across the world.**

One of Kardashian West and Kanye's early public appearances as a couple was at a Los Angeles Lakers basketball game.

women's bodies. Women can face pressure from society to look skinny. But Kardashian West often liked to show off her body's curves.

Kardashian West said her **selfies** showed how proud she was of her body. As a child, she felt insecure about her body shape. But as an adult, she challenged the idea that women had to be skinny to be beautiful.

Kardashian West also used social media to promote products. Some were her own. In December 2015, the month Saint was born, Kardashian West released an app called KIMOJI. It featured custom **emojis** called "Kimojis." Many of the emojis represented famous moments from Kardashian West's life. Every few weeks, the app released new designs. Kardashian West used Instagram to advertise these new emojis to fans.

Companies also paid Kardashian West to **endorse** their products on social media. Often, this meant she posed with the product in a selfie. Kardashian West's popularity and influence drove fans to buy what she promoted. One **marketing**

SNAPCHAT STAR

In 2016, Kardashian said that each of her Snapchat posts were watched by 8 to 9 million people. This is three times the number of people who regularly watched *Keeping Up with the Kardashians*!

London's famous wax museum Madame Tussauds features a wax model of Kardashian West. The model is taking a selfie with a functioning phone!

expert said Kardashian's posts could help products sell out immediately!

Social media was a huge part of Kardashian West's brand. Her posts let people into her personal life. They also kept fans up-to-date on Kardashian West's favorite products and trends. But there was a dark side to Kardashian West's openness on social media.

CHAPTER 7

SOCIAL MEDIA SCARE

In October 2016, social media played a role in a terrifying experience for Kardashian West. On a trip to Paris, France, she was robbed in her hotel room. The thieves left with her jewelry. Although physically unharmed, Kardashian West was deeply shaken. It was later revealed that the robbers found her location through her social media posts. Information she shared with fans had been used to target her.

Kardashian West's life slowed down after the robbery. For months, the normally open star stopped posting on social media. She was rarely seen in public. Kardashian West was nervous that if she went out, her home would be robbed. When she was seen in public, Kardashian West wore little jewelry.

While the robbery was scary, Kardashian West said that she learned from it. The incident made her reflect on how much she shared with her social media followers. In a later interview, Kardashian West revealed that she no

Police and reporters gathered outside the building where Kardashian West was robbed in Paris. The robbers had stolen millions of dollars' worth of her jewelry.

longer posted her location in real time. "I just don't like people knowing my every move," she said.

The robbery did not permanently silence Kardashian West. In fact, she was ready to launch a new chapter in her career. In the coming year, Kardashian West would return to social media with a special announcement.

BEAUTY BUSINESS

In 2017, Kardashian West used social media to introduce her new beauty company. That June, she launched KKW Beauty. Kardashian West had been busy developing easy-to-use **contour** kits. Contouring was one of her **signature** makeup styles. She used it to shade areas of her face to define her features.

In the past, Kardashian West lent her name to products and got money in return. But until KKW Beauty, she had never run her own business. Kardashian West was inspired by her husband to make this change. Kanye believed that owning his projects let him stay true to himself. Kardashian West soon agreed. She said it was worth it to work hard on something she owned.

Kardashian West's contour kits were popular from the start. When they launched in June 2017, they sold out in less than three hours. The kits brought in an estimated $100 million in their first year. Though popular, the kits got mixed reviews. So, Kardashian West took suggestions from fans on social media. In an interview, she said that fans were helping to build her brand!

Kardashian West's half-sister Kylie Jenner (*left*) also runs a popular makeup business. It is called Kylie Cosmetics.

CHAPTER 9

KEEPING UP WITH KIM

With her new beauty brand, Kardashian West grew even more famous. Her company grew as well. After the success of the **contour** kits, KKW Beauty expanded to include more makeup. In 2018, the brand began selling eye shadow, lipstick, and more.

The coming year was busy for Kardashian West. Her third child, Chicago, was born in January 2018. In April, Kardashian West launched a fragrance line, KKW Body. The brand is true to her positive outlook on all body types. Kardashian featured women of different sizes in promotional photos on social media. The perfume bottles are even shaped like Kardashian's body!

Also in 2018, Kardashian West became an **activist**. The previous year, she had learned about Alice Johnson. Johnson had been serving a life sentence in prison since 1996 for a nonviolent crime. Since then, Johnson had turned her life around. Kardashian West thought Johnson's life sentence was unfair.

BIO BASICS

NAME: Kim Kardashian West

NICKNAME: Kiki

BIRTH: October 21, 1980, Beverly Hills, California

SPOUSES: Damon Thomas (2000-2004); Kris Humphries (2011); Kanye West (2014-present)

CHILDREN: North, Saint, Chicago, and Psalm

FAMOUS FOR: her reality TV show, social media following, and makeup business

ACHIEVEMENTS: starred on a popular reality TV show for 15 seasons and counting; gained millions of followers on social media; ran a successful makeup business

In May 2018, Kardashian West met with President Donald Trump at the White House. She urged the president to pardon Johnson from her life sentence. Kardashian West's efforts were successful. On June 6, 2018, Trump pardoned Johnson. After Johnson's release, Kardashian West expressed interest in continuing to work toward criminal justice reform.

In early 2019, Kardashian West had more exciting news to share with her fans. She and Kanye announced they were expecting a fourth child that spring. In May, they welcomed a second son, Psalm. Kardashian West's growing family continued to draw the attention of millions.

Kardashian West found fame on reality TV. But she has become famous for much more. Today, she is one of the most followed people on social media. She is also an **entrepreneur** and lifestyle icon.

 You can say a lot of things about me, but you cannot say I don't work hard. I don't sing. I don't dance. I don't act. But I am not lazy.

Like Kardashian West, President Trump is active on social media. In a Twitter post, he called his visit with Kardashian West a "great meeting."

Kardashian West's ability to connect with fans around the world has made her successful. As she once said playfully, "Not bad for a girl with no talent!"

TIMELINE

2014
Kardashian and West get married. Kardashian changes her name to Kim Kardashian West.

1980
Kimberly Noel Kardashian is born in Beverly Hills, California, on October 21.

2013
In June, Kardashian has a daughter, North, with Kanye West.

2007
Keeping Up with the Kardashians premieres on TV.

May 2015
Kardashian West releases *Selfish*, a book of selfies.

December 2015
Kardashian West gives birth to a son, Saint. The same month, she releases an emoji app called KIMOJI.

January 2018

Kardashian West welcomes a second daughter, Chicago.

May 2018

Kardashian West urges President Trump to release Alice Johnson from prison. Johnson is released one month later.

2017

Kardashian West launches KKW Beauty.

2016

Kardashian West is robbed in her Paris hotel room. The incident causes her to reflect on what she posts on social media.

2019

Kardashian West welcomes her second son, Psalm, in May.

GLOSSARY

activist—a person who takes direct action in support of or in opposition to an issue that causes disagreement.

cancer—any of a group of often deadly diseases marked by harmful changes in the normal growth of cells. Cancer can spread and destroy healthy tissues and organs.

client—a person who hires or uses the services of a professional of some type.

contour—the general form or outline of something. Contouring is shaping the general form or outline of something.

emoji—a small symbol or picture that can be typed in an email, a text, or an online post.

endorse—to publicly recommend a product or service in exchange for money.

entrepreneur—one who organizes, manages, and accepts the risks of a business or an enterprise.

ethic—a set of principles governing an individual or group.

footage—action recorded on film or videotape.

marketing—the process of advertising or promoting something so people will want to buy it.

petition—a formal request to a person of authority.

potential—a quality that someone or something has that can be developed or used.

premiere—to have a first performance or exhibition.

ratings—estimated numbers of people watching a TV show.

selfie—an image of oneself taken by oneself using a digital camera, especially for posting on social networks.

signature—serving to set apart or identify an individual, group, or company.

socialite—someone who is well-known and social among wealthy people.

transgender—having a gender identity that differs from the one associated with one's sex at birth.

ONLINE RESOURCES

Booklinks
NONFICTION NETWORK
FREE! ONLINE NONFICTION RESOURCES

To learn more about Kim Kardashian West, please visit **abdobooklinks.com** or scan this QR code. These links are routinely monitored and updated to provide the most current information available.

INDEX